ANCIENT MESOPOTAMIA

2nd Grade History Book
Children's Ancient History Edition

Speedy Publishing LLC
40 E. Main St. #1156
Newark, DE 19711
www.speedypublishing.com

Mesopotamia is part of a larger area that archeologists call the Fertile Crescent.

Ancient Mesopotamia refers to the place where humans first formed civilizations.

Mesopotamia is the name of an ancient region which means the land between two rivers.

It was in Mesopotamia that people first began to live in large cities and created governments.

Mesopotamia is often referred to as the 'Cradle of Civilization'.

Most of Ancient Mesopotamia was located in what today is the country of Iraq.

Mesopotamia included a region of approximately 300 miles long by 150 miles wide.

13675
Mosul
1385
Aleppo
Khābūr
Euphrates
Latakia
SYRIA
Tharthār Depression
10131
Damascus
Sea of Galilee
SYRIAN DESERT
5905
Jabal 'Unayzah
3068
'Ammān
3510
2329

Teheran
Namak
Lake
Asadābād Pass
11073
7241
Z a g r o s
Diyala
Dez
Qom
P E R
Karkheh
Isfa
Zard Kūh
14921
14100
Kārūn
Euphrates
Hawr al
Ḩammār
Basra
Shaṭṭ al
Arab
Ṣaḥrā' al Ḩijārah
1212

The heart of Mesopotamia lies between the two rivers in southern Iraq.

The land is fertile and there is plenty of water around the major two rivers to allow for irrigation and farming.

Mesopotamia's major cities included Baghdad, Babylon and Nippur.

Babylon was the capital of Mesopotamia. At times the Babylonians would create vast empires that ruled much of the Middle East.

At the center of each major city was a temple to the city's god called a ziggurat.

Each city in Mesopotamia had a primary god. The ziggurat showed that the city was dedicated to that god.

Most people lived in mud brick homes. The mud brick worked as a good insulator to keep the homes a bit cooler in the summer and warmer in the winter.

They enjoyed music at festivals including drums, lyres, flutes, and harps. They also enjoyed sports such as boxing and wrestling.

As Sumerian towns grew into cities, the people needed a way to keep track of business transactions, ownership rights, and government records.

The first form of ancient writing was invented by the Sumerians. They wrote on tablets and drew pictures which represented ideas or objects to keep their records.

The Ancient Mesopotamians were experimenting with ways to count, measure, and solve mathematical problems.

The ancient Mesopotamians did not use money, so they developed a system of weights to buy and sell things.

Visit
BABY PROFESSOR
EDUCATION KIDS
www.BabyProfessorBooks.com
to download Free Baby Professor eBooks
and view our catalog of new and exciting
Children's Books

www.ingramcontent.com/pod-product-compliance
Lightning Source LLC
LaVergne TN
LVHW060509170826
845677LV00026B/1705
9798869449115